Table of Contents

1. Introduction

If you are anything like me, you probably know very little about 3D printing – although are very interested to find out more. In this book I give you a basic overview of the history, process, and opportunities and just how you go about the process of 3D printing.

In 1984, the first working 3D printer was created at 3D Systems Corporation when Chuck Hall turned the concept into reality. More than 30 years later, objects are "printed" in three dimensions with thousands of thin layers of various materials. The 3D printer closely resembles a document printer since the carriage that applies the materials moves across the surface in a series of repetitive passes. As the layers build, the platform is lowered less than one millimeter at a time to leave sufficient space for layers to be added to the top of the object.

2. Overview of 3D printing

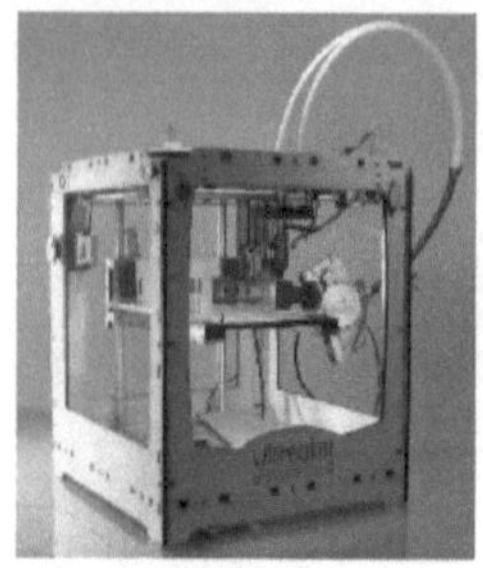

The 3D printing process falls within the broader category of additive manufacturing, which requires successive layers of material to be stacked in different shapes. A solid object is built from a digital model in three dimensions of virtually any shape. Traditional machining techniques follow subtractive processes where excess material is removed from a solid piece of material through cutting, drilling or sanding.

3D printers, or materials printers, perform the 3D printing process with digital technology. A detailed design is created from a computer concept or scanned object and then sent to the printer. The size of the object determines the amount of material and number of hours required to complete the building process.

Since the turn of the 21st century, interest in 3D printing has grown exponentially. The cost of 3D printers has dropped sufficiently to allow companies in many industries to embrace 3D printing technology. Countless uses have been discovered for prototyping and distributive manufacturing. Creating unique objects is no longer cost- prohibitive since the design and material can be transformed into the desired shape for an acceptable cost.

3. 3D Printing Terminology & Evolution of 3D Printers

COMMON 3D PRINTING TERMINOLOGY

Certain words are used to convey specific meaning in the 3D printing realm. Appropriate definitions allow the reader to understand the concepts without confusion.

• Additive manufacturing – A sequential layering process used to create solid objects of various materials.
• Rapid prototyping – Preproduction modeling where an exact replica of the conceptual model is produced.
• Rapid manufacturing – Full-scale production where high volume creation of the object is performed.
• Subtractive manufacturing – Removal of excess material from a block that is drilled, shaved or filed into the correct size and shape.
• Fabrication – Joining of plates, sheets or forging using rivets, screws and welds to hold materials together.
• Machining – Generation of exact shapes through high-precision subtractive methods where filing, turning, milling and grinding is used in subtractive techniques.

EVOLUTION OF 3D PRINTERS

Prototypes have been one of the most expensive requirements of the manufacturing process. The invention of 3D printing has revolutionized prototyping since a unique object can be designed through computer-aided design and fed into the 3D printing software. Visionaries at MIT wanted to place on-demand prototyping within reach of designers and engineers in every industry. The advent of 3D printers would follow the document printers that have changed the way every industry presents information to the world. Speed, accuracy, affordability, usability and color were the highest priorities for the industry's 3D printers.

• 1st Generation – Basic materials are "printed" in layers to replicate the concept object into a 3D object. Colors were basic, and speed was moderate.
• 2nd Generation – Improved speed set the next generation of 3D printers apart from the earlier models. As interest grew, the prices dropped into the affordable range for companies in dozens of industries. Rapid prototyping in more colors and materials was possible.
• 3rd Generation – Ease of use separates the latest generation of 3D printers. Self-contained units complete the entire process through print and depowder. The result is a 3D printer that is convenient and can be located virtually anywhere. Larger printers have become more affordable, and users are able to create larger objects.

4. Sources of 3D virtual modals

The 3D printer must receive instructions that will be followed to turn the series of printed layers into the desired three-dimensional object. Various input types are available to transform a conceptual object into a 3D object that can be used in many different ways, such as working components, prototypes or replicas.

• Modeling – Virtual blueprints can be used to create input for the 3D printer. These plans, which come from CAD or animation modeling software, are reduced to a series of "slices" that make up the digital cross-sections of the virtual object. The layers will be produced from the materials inside the 3D printer. An exact replica of the virtual object is "printed" on the platform, or build bed, inside the printer.

Through this method, the printer receives information in the standard STL file format that is the standard data interface between the CAD software and 3D printer. Triangular facets are used to represent the exact shape of the part in the STL file. A 3D scanner will generate a PLY input file for the 3D printer. Full color specifications are stored in VRML or WRL format.

• Image-based modeling – In this user-assisted approach, the 3D build specifications are created through a series of pictures of the object to be replicated. Common uses for this approach include models of buildings. Through photogrammetry, photos are assembled into a series of instructions that a 3D printer can follow to "print" a scale model of the structure. Photographs from multiple angles are used to generate the virtual image.

• Scanner – An existing object can be duplicated when a 3D scanner is used to record the dimensions. 3D printing software offers the user options, which include scaling and color enhancement. Shiny and transparent objects present challenges to the scanner since light from the scanner does not follow the outline of the object.

Common applications for the 3D scanner include orthotics, prosthetics, industrial design, prototyping, reverse engineering, inspection, quality control and recording cultural artifacts.

5. Materials for use in 3D printing applications, & Acquiring materials

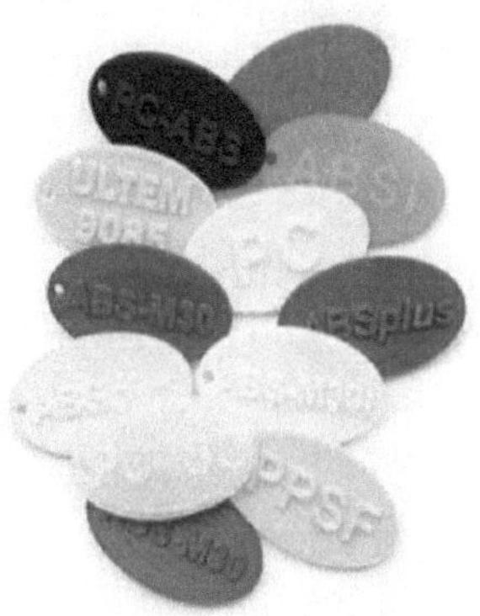

MATERIALS FOR USE IN 3D PRINTING APPLICATIONS

3D printing supports the use of many different materials that can be used to produce objects. Each application requires special care in acquiring sufficient material to complete the print steps without stopping. 3D printers vary in the types of materials that can be used, so the specifications must be known prior to purchasing the equipment.

These surprising materials can be used for 3D printing:

• Salt – The abundance of salt around the globe opens doors of possibility in 3D printing. White and translucent properties make salt attractive and interesting for use in replicating art objects. Post processing increases strength and durability of the object.

• Cement polymer – This strong, rigid material can include fiber reinforcement to become stronger than standard concrete. Industrial applications are limitless with this compound.

• Nylon – Tiny layers of nylon produced from a 3D printer will reveal each detail in the object. Colors of nylon are true to the design. Nylon is strong and flexible for use in many different applications, including art objects with tiny details.

• Wood – Made from recycled and reclaimed wood, this 3D printing material is combined with cellulose material. The printed object will have moderate strength and a certain level of translucency. Fiber reinforcement is possible to increase the physical strength of the object. The look and feel of medium-density fiberboard is common in printed wood.

• Resin – Printed objects made of resin have luster and sheen. Strength is an important quality for many delicate designs that appear to be fragile. Intricate designs of resin can be hollow without losing strength. Colors remain vibrant. This less expensive material is used in numerous applications, including replicating art objects.

• Concrete – Objects that will encounter moisture and outdoor use can be 3D printed with concrete. Post processing, such as sand blasting, creates a smooth surface that is strong, water-resistant and attractive.

• ABS – As the most common filament, ABS has become a standard material in architectural applications. During the printing process, the bed must be heated to maintain pliability in the ABS for each layer to adhere to the object. Removal from the bed can be especially challenging since the ABS tends to warp at the edge that touches the bed. A strong odor is produced when the ABS is heated, so proper ventilation is required.

• PLA – Another filament material that will correct many of the challenges presented by ABS. The lower extrusion temperature does not require a heated printing bed. The glossier finish of PLA is attractive and the material does not warp as dramatically. PLA is somewhat brittle but strong, as well as biodegradable and odorless.

• PVA – This least common plastic is used as the support material when printing with dual-extruding printers. The low melting point and similar texture makes it easy to print. PVA can be dissolved away from the object through simple submersion. Sensitivity to water means this 3D printer filament must be stored carefully to prevent ruin. All PVA material must be sealed and stored in a cool, dry location. In humid climates, extra precaution must be taken to preserve the PVA for use.

ACQUIRING MATERIALS FOR 3D PRINTING

Online suppliers offer sample kits to allow the 3D printing enthusiast to determine which material is appropriate for the object. Prices are provided for cubic centimeters of each material. The customer can request assistance for determining how much material would be needed for the item to be printed. Support material should be acquired at the same time to ensure the two materials will work well together in the 3D printer.

6. Basic 3D printing concepts

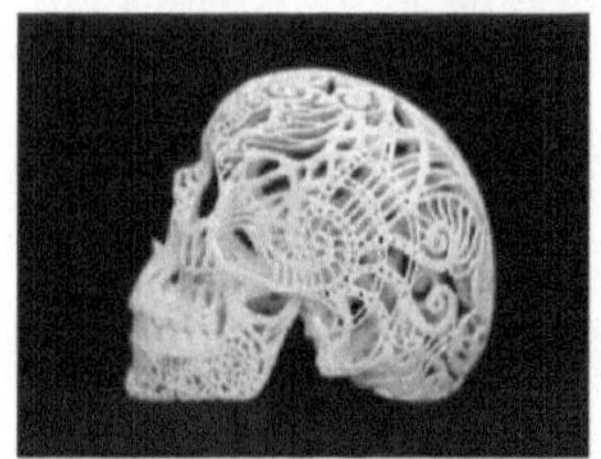

Understanding 3D printing is possible when the entire process follows the same basic steps each time. The object that is produced from the 3D printer originates in a computer or in the real world. Each step of the process is required to achieve the desired result.

• Modeling - 3D print designs are made up of an extensive series of slices in a digital cross-section. Computer software converts the conceptual object into an understandable format for the 3D printer to use. Changes to the image can be performed prior to finalizing the design. Size, dimension and color changes will be recorded within the software before the design is converted into the format required for 3D printing. Decisions concerning the appropriate material used to create the final object will be made during this phase.

• Printing – The finalized object design file will be sent to the printer to initiate the entire series of 3D printing steps. An .STL file is stored in the printer's memory as each layer of liquid, paper, powder or sheet material is stacked to build the object according to the exact specifications in the cross section. Instructions in the design file will inform the printer of the material qualities to ensure the temperature, layer thickness and finishing times are correct. Virtual objects from the software are assembled as the miniscule layers form a solid object. This slice-by-slice approach supports the creation of almost any geometric feature or design shape.

• Finishing – 3D printing materials require sufficient periods of time to cure and dry. Removal of the object prior to proper curing will cause the object to change under the pressure of a hand or its own weight. 3D printers are equipped with dryers that produce perfect temperatures inside the printing chamber to cause the materials to harden. The chamber will return to room temperature as the curing process is completed.

HOW THE 3D PRINTING PROCESS WORKS

=.=

Fascinating ideas that appeared on the platform of a replicator in science fiction TV shows were foretelling events that have become possible in the 21st century. 3D printers are designed to accept a conceptual idea that exists in a computer image and create a physical object. The computer model is created in computer-aided design software that records exact dimensions oriented on the X, Y and Z axes.

• Standard file formats include .STL, .PLY, .ZPR and .3DS, which come from the various software packages. The 3D printer will convert the files into instructions that are followed to create the object.

• Every side of the object must be solid because the layers will be "printed" on top of each other. Gaps will cause layers to collapse and the object's shape will be compromised.

• Gaps in the final object will be filled with support material, which is intended to be removed from the final object after printing. 3D printers will combine support material with other materials in the exact proportion to print the object in the real world. After the object is finished, the support material is rinsed away in water.

• Users have the option of increasing or decreasing the object's size prior to performing the print cycle. The 3D printer's platform, or print bed, present the limits for the final object size, which includes the height of the object.

• The printer will replicate the object through a series of layers that are printed one on top of the other until the physical object is constructed in the 3D printer's build chamber.

7. 3D Printing advantages and features

Designs for objects that have never before existed used to take weeks of months to create through subtraction processes. Multiple iterations where changes were made added time to the design process of every object before the first manufacturing process was initiated. Delays were expensive since revenue was not being generated during the costly design phase.

Today, an engineer can open the CAD software, draw a component on the screen with the stylus and add specifications. The virtual object exists in a three dimensional format within the computer's memory. Adjustments to size, color and shape can be made according to the project's requirements. Consultations can occur in the same room or around the globe in real time. The result is a component that will fulfill the need following the 3D printing process.

The entire team realizes significant benefits throughout the 3D printing cycle:

• Design cycles are significantly shorter;
• Superior products can be offered in the marketplace before competitors know what is coming;
• R&D budgets are optimized;
• Accuracy of every design is improved;
• Costly mistakes are eliminated from the process;
• Innovative ideas are triggered throughout the concept stage since the component is visible;

• Quality improves since the team can recognize flaws; and
• Collaboration has never been easier between the teams: sales, marketing, engineering and executive.

3D PRINTERS OFFER POWERFUL FEATURES

=-=

Technology continues to advance at the speed of light. Those who use 3D printers anticipate the new models since each version offers remarkable new features. Greater capability enhances the ways that 3D printing can be incorporated into various industrial and private activities.

• Speed – 3D printer speed continues to increase because of the materials that dry faster. Each layer of a 3D design can be applied with rapid passes of the carriage through print heads that cover as much as one-half inch of surface. The temperature inside the chamber is optimal for each material used. Objects that once required multiple days to "print" can be finished in a matter of hours. Improved speed is supported through larger printer memory and accessing speeds.

• Affordability – Large 3D printers were once prohibitively expensive. Popularity in 3D printing has encouraged many industries to embrace the technology. Supplies for 3D printers are made of common manufacturing materials that are easy to acquire. Each process within the printer is self-contained to reduce waste. Objects can be made for approximately two to three dollars per cubic inch. Affordable 3D printer models are available with capabilities to suit large or small firms. Even expensive 3D printers can provide acceptable return on investment since manufacturing, prototyping and modeling costs are reduced substantially.

• Ease of use – 3D printing firmware directs the printer's actions through the entire self-contained printing process. The standard digital pattern, which is in an .STL file format, provides specification for each layer in the virtual design. The user loads the proper material for the printer to use as the physical object is created on the print bed. 3D printers are designed to be as user-friendly as a document printer is. A professional office environment can support the addition of a 3D printer. The build process runs without supervision to allow the user to go about other duties until the entire design is built.

• Accuracy – Designers want to know that the object created in the CAD software will be replicated exactly in the 3D printer. Print-head design, build materials and mechanical design work together to provide precision in the conversion from the conceptual design to the physical object. Details that are tiny, such as 0.004 inch, and walls as thin as 0.02 inch can be created in any material the printer will support. 3D printers are comparable in accuracy to the injection molding technique that has been used for decades.

• Color – CAD software is able to assign colors within the design that follow important industry standards. 3D printers are advancing to support the effort to apply colors that will communicate Finite Element Analysis, or FEA, results, separate parts of an assembly or manufacturing steps. Logos, text or an engineering label on the part can be printed for easy identification. Third generation 3D printers are able to convert color from the RGB scale on the computer to the CMYK color value printers use. 3D printers have the capability to place the requested color in the correct area of the design.

8. 3D Printing could be a game changer....

Since 1984, rapid prototyping was confined to engineering labs where the 3D printer could create a flimsy replica from a CAD design. Limitations in the plastics and metals used in the 3D printers created poor-quality objects that would never leave the lab. Subsequent steps were required to create a high-quality model for use in various applications. 3D Systems recognized this shortcoming in the field and set out to improve the materials that would be used in 3D printers. Nanocomposites were created of various plastics or powdered metals. 3D printers are able to stack fine layers of the material according to the CAD designs and create end products that can perform the desired function.

Sturdy materials offer endless possibilities for various applications that currently require suppliers and stores to stock an inventory of products that consumers wish to purchase. Instead, a 3D printer would "print" the desired object for the consumer. Inventories of finished goods would be replaced with raw materials that are ready for use in the 3D printer. Increased speed in each generation of 3D printers will reduce the amount of time required to print the object.

Some of the possible uses include:

• Auto parts for any make or model

• Airplane parts that would be available at any airport in the country when needed.

• Furniture that is "printed" according to the customer's request.

• Medical prosthesis in the correct size for the patient without months of waiting.

• Dental apparatus created for use in the individual's mouth according to the dimensions specified.

Discussions concerning copyrights and design ownership have surfaced since the 3D printer would use a design belongs to a legal entity. Use of designs would have to follow certain guidelines to prevent chaos in the economy.

Economies of scale are undermined when the 3D printer can create a unique object without regard for massive set-up sequences that govern the manufacturing process of an entire factory. A single item could be produced upon request as long as the appropriate materials were available for the 3D printer. Consumers would have access to an endless selection of on-demand items for purchase. Retailers would emphasize materials for use in building each product instead of carrying an extensive inventory of items that may never sell.

9. Applications for 3D printing

When paired with a 3D scanner, the 3D printer becomes a replicator for objects that would fit in the print chamber of the printer. A small object made of resin could be scanned and recreated through rapid prototyping. The result is an exact duplicate. Art objects could be scanned for safekeeping in the event that a natural disaster destroyed the original. Endless possibilities arise through the creative use of the 3D printing technology.

Additive manufacturing, the basis of 3D printing, is advancing into many fields where subtractive methods were used exclusively in the past. Lead time is reduced when a prototype for a new product can be drawn on a computer screen, refined and "printed" in a matter of hours. Obvious changes are occurring in standard applications that include design visualization, CAD, prototype creation, metal casting, education, architecture, healthcare, retail and entertainment.

• Rapid manufacturing – Final manufacturing processes require materials that are now available for 3D printers. Inexpensive production of small quantities of items will reduce costs and waste. Current processes within the rapid manufacturing realm remain unproven. Materials must be available in proper quantities to allow consumers to acquire affordable raw materials for use in the 3D printer.

• Mass customization – Companies offer services where a basic design is modified to match the customer's needs. Web-based customization allows the customer to make changes that will be printed as unique objects. A custom cell phone case is possible when the customer orders through the website.

• Mass production – Printing large quantities of one design is a limitation in the 3D printing field. Several models of fused-filament 3D printers have multiple extruder heads inside. Various colors, different polymers or multiple prints of the same design are possible through these advanced machines.

Multiple instance production, which requires lower capital investments, is possible. Multi-material machines are available for producing multiple copies of the same part.

10. Industries using 3D printing

Additive manufacturing techniques offer new ways to perform various functions in many different industries. Innovative approaches are devised when barriers to production are encountered. In some industries, the design phase calls for rapid creation of components that support the next phase of a process. Other industries can utilize 3D printing to produce final products using advanced materials. The possibilities are endless.

• Architecture – Traditional methods of creating a scale model have always included foam board and glue that would be used to complete a tedious process that would require weeks of hard work. The result was a delicate model that was difficult to transport without damage. 3D scanners can record the dimensions of an existing structure to create the digital images that will be transformed into a standard format file for the 3D printer. Building plans and virtual blueprints are transformed into digital designs in the 3D printing software. The 3D printer builds the scale model in-house where the design remains confidential. Printed scale models are sturdy and resilient.

• Automotive – Functional parts were once created from subtractive processes that required dyes forged from steel. Mistakes were expensive since the entire process had to start over from the top. Today, functional parts can be created and tested immediately after the curative process is completed in the 3D printer. After-market parts have always presented expensive challenges for the automakers. Functional 3D designs are provided for replacement parts that can be used when needed. During the design phase of new car models, the engine block or gearbox can be designed in the computer and sent to the 3D printer for fabrication in a matter of hours. Mistakes are avoided, which reduces costs. Custom car and motorcycle builders are using 3D printing to fabricate unique designs that include fairings, fenders and instrument clusters.

• Manufacturing – Components for virtually any machine can be improved through CAD design and additive manufacturing. A 3D printer that is capable of using powdered metals can create a strong part that will replace a broken one. Repairs are easier than ever when the designs are available upon request to the customer in almost any location. An extensive inventory of spare parts is no longer required when the 3D printer can produce comparable parts.

• Consumer products – Additive manufacturing in-house prevents competitors from discovering the new products that are in development. Unique product details can be evaluated after the 3D printing process has brought the concept into the real world. Kitchen products, electronics packaging and toys are some of the most obvious candidates for 3D printing. Modeling these products allows companies to ask for consumer input prior to mass production processes that are expensive when the consumer is not interested, and the product does not sell.

• Educational – Students in many professional disciplines are learning the essential steps in the 3D design and printing processes. Innovation in the classroom has offered many solutions to corporations whose R&D budgets are limited. Real-life experiences enhance the education experience and bring real-world needs into the educational system. The result is employees with a better understanding of what employers require.

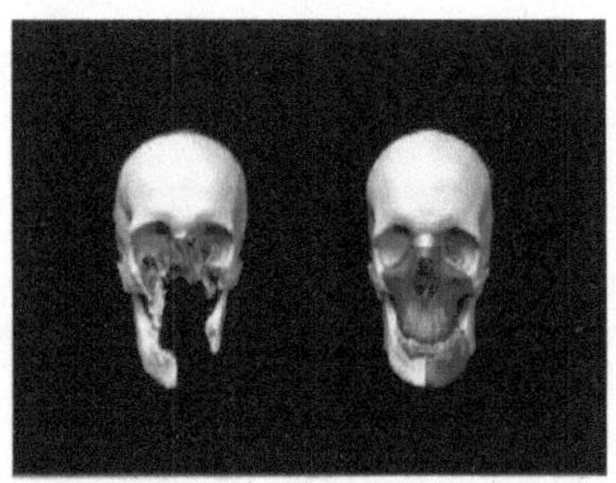

• Medical – Subtractive manufacturing has dominated the creation of surgical instruments whenever new tools are needed. Slow design processes cause concern since lives could be saved through the use of the new instruments. Instead, additive manufacturing removes the extra steps required to refine designs before the instruments are fabricated in metal. Prosthetics can be modeled to fit the patient based on the measurements provided in the CAD software. The perfect fit is achieved when the 3D printer produces the exact object in a matter of hours. Patients will receive a new limb that fits without having to wait for cumbersome manufacturing processes.

• Dental – Old dental procedures required multiple-step processes where the dentist made a mold of the patient's mouth in clay. A crown would be made by hand and refined through sanding procedures while the patient waited many days or weeks for the crown. Today, the dentist will use a 3D scanner in a hand-held wand that was created in the 3M labs. The digital image of the patient's mouth is used to create a CAD image of the crown. The 3D printer "prints" the crown in dental compounds that will last for decades. On the next business day, the dentist can finish the procedure. Patients are able to enjoy eating normally after a couple of days of discomfort.

• Artistic – Museums are scanning art objects and storing the images for recreating a replica if one is lost in a natural disaster. Originals can never be replaced, but beautiful objects can be created when the 3D printing technology is employed in the proper situations. Artists are using this technology to bring concepts to life in the real world without struggling with conceptual drawings and sets of renderings, which have always been difficult to read. Non-traditional materials are changing the face of artistry through 3D printing.

• Culinary – Simple 3D printers have been built to allow a chef to ice a cake in intricate patterns with icing squeezed through a standard icing envelope mounted on the printer carriage. The arms of the printer move in lateral motion across the surface of the cake according to the computer's instructions. Steady hands are no longer required to be a talented cake decorator.

11. Controversial uses and advanced ideas in 3D Printing

Any technology that was originally created to solve a problem has the potential of meeting a controversial need as well. In the United States, gun control surfaced after a series of incidents where high-capacity magazines were used to kill innocent men, women and children. Shortly thereafter, CAD designs for guns and magazines were generated and uploaded to various websites for anyone to use. The response from the State Department was swift, but futile. The responsibility for proper use of any technology rests with the user. Legislating wise use of a CAD gun blueprint is comparable to attempting to confiscate the 300 million guns that exist in the U.S.

Some people would argue that the 3D printing of human cells, skin and tissue is questionable. Precision is essential for the medical applications where 3D printing is revolutionizing procedures. Ethics will be questioned if the source of the materials crosses moral boundaries. Every researcher and medical professional must consider the value of human life in each decision.

Intellectual property laws have surfaced as a primary concern when a CAD file can be shared between any number of users. Patents, copyrights and trademarks are attached to the three types of intellectual property.

• Patent – protects how something works from duplication and lasts up to 25 years, which varies by jurisdiction

• Copyright – protects artistic works and covers the artist's life plus 70 years

• Trademark – a recognizable sign, expression or design that identifies a product or service from the unique source. The owner can be a person, business or legal entity.

Advocates of 3D printing practices offer open source designs for 3D printers to encourage others to build a device and participate in the practice. Opponents raise concerns that property laws must be observed when producing products that fall under patents, copyrights and trademarks. The freedom to "print" virtually any object from the CAD design with proper raw materials must be balanced with respect for the existing commerce laws.

ADVANCED IDEAS FOR 3D PRINTING

=-=-=-=-=-=-=-=-=-=-=-=-=-=-=-=-=-=

As interest in 3D printing expands, innovation is reaching areas where experts envision more science-related uses for the technology. Subtractive techniques could never replicate the minute details in some of these areas.

• Paleontology – reconstruct fossils from digital images and 3D scans

• Archeology – replicate ancient, or priceless, artifacts without risking damage through conventional methods
• Forensic pathology – reconstruct bones and body parts for examination

• Crime scene investigation – recreate evidence that is damaged

Creation of the CAD files for use in the 3D printer allows the specialist to preserve one-of-a-kind items to prevent permanent loss. Scans and digital images can be enhanced, scaled and modified for any number of uses in each category. Improvements in the raw materials available for 3D printing remove barriers from the expansion of 3D printing applications. Ideas associated with unique uses can be hindered if the available materials do not yet exist for use in the 3D printer.

TOY STORES COULD DISAPPEAR

Extensive selections of plastics available for use in 3D printers could make mass production of toys obsolete. Shopping for toys could involve design selection, downloading the CAD file to the 3D printer, loading the proper materials and "printing" the new toy in the comfort of home. Children would dunk the new toy in water to wash away the support materials and have a new action figure in a matter of hours.

The purchase of the CAD file would cover the cost of designing the toy. Companies would offer packages that include the appropriate materials for each toy. Consumers would wait for the materials to arrive and finish the process on the personal 3D printer.

These revolutionary ideas could become reality in the not-too-distance future.

12. Home Models - 3d Printers and how to make money

In the past six years, commercial 3D printers have dropped in price from $30,000 for the least expensive model to approximately $2,000. Broader interest in industrial applications has created interest for the home enthusiast, too. An Internet search for "3D printer plans" returns a list of open source plans that can be built for $400-$500. Plans for the printer include instructions for building some of the components for the printer itself. Interest in 3D printing at home will cause exponential growth in the applications.

Interested 3D printer enthusiasts should read the plans for multiple 3D printers prior to embarking on the mission to build one. Each design varies in quality and complexity with respect to other designs. A simple printer will be limited in the types of builds that are possible. Size limitations are important considerations for the person who has a specific use in mind prior to building a 3D printer. The build platform and distance from the print carriage will limit the size of objects that can be built on each model of printer.

Pre-built home 3D printers have been available since 2012. The cost of the most common model is $2,000, which is affordable for people with specific uses in mind. Costs will continue to drop as more people purchase a 3D printer for use in the home, shop and office.

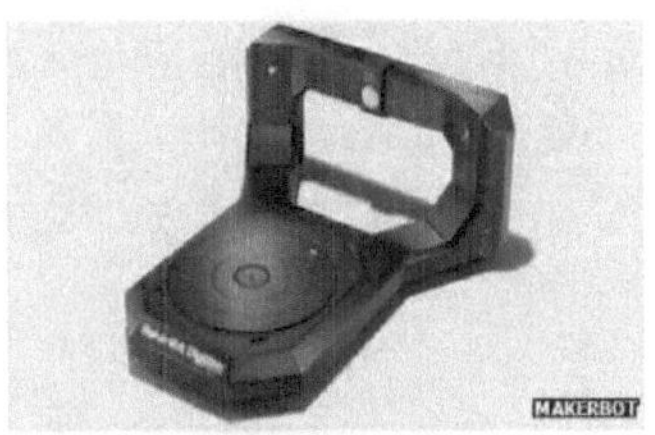

Just very recently there has been a desktop version to be available from October of 2013 (above). Demand for the machine appeared to overload the company's website when it went on sale on 22.8.13. The Digitizer by Makerbot is the latest product looking to bring 3D printing to the masses - but many experts are skeptical. The makers state that expectations should not be too high. The machine is designed to allow the replication of objects without any need for the user to learn any 3D modeling software or have any other relative expertise.

Depending on the size it would estimate you could print a small to medium size object in 13-20 minutes. It will cost US200.

MAKE MONEY WITH 3D PRINTING

=-=-=-=-=-=-=-=-=-=-=-=-=-=-=-=-=-=

Hackerspaces and fablabs are sprouting up around the globe to fill the gap between commercial 3D printers that cost hundreds of thousands of dollars and the simple home models that have limited capabilities. Creative individuals have noticed a gap in the marketplace and decided to embark on business ventures such as these:

• Two men decided to pack up an economy car with two laptops and four 3D printers for a journey across the country. At each stop, the duo will design, test and produce an item that is sold at a fair price to the consumer. Toys, jewelry and cell phone accessories are popular items that can be printed in a matter of hours.

• Another designer embarked on his mission to create custom minifigs for Lego figurines. Discontinued hats were the first need that launched his business on Shapeways where he has sold more than 5,000 items.

• A passion for toy robots turned into a business for one pair of entrepreneurs. The customer visits the website, selects certain options and determines the size of the robot, which is delivered right to the consumer's door.

• Visits to a 3D printing website can yield innovative solutions to simple or complex challenges. Web-based software allows the customer to design an object and send it to the 3D printer. These services are meeting needs for individuals and customers alike.

• 3D printing businesses are growing rapidly through infusions of investment cash from friends and family members. Small businesses recognize the value of 3D printing for certain applications and can contact 3D printing company to fill specific needs without buying the equipment. More of these businesses will sprout up as needs are defined.

13. Limitations of 3D printing

Advances in 3D scanning, CAD software designs and 3D printer capabilities will resolve some of the limitations and barriers encountered in 3D printing. Certain items cannot be created because the materials are not available, or the object is too complex. Some specific examples illustrate limitations in real-world terms.

• Objects with complicated inner-workings cannot be replicated on a 3D printer, including industrial 3D printer models.

• Items made of multiple materials must be assembled from components printed of one material each. One component made of multiple materials cannot be built with a 3D printer.

• Moving parts present challenges unless two separate components can be printed individually and fit together later.

• An item that requires a perfectly smooth surface that will touch another surface must be "machined-off" manually for moving parts.

• Objects that have an overhanging edge present a challenge because of the quantity of support materials that are necessary to support the overhang.

General Limitations in 3D Printing Technology

Additive manufacturing allows designers and engineers to create affordable prototypes in short periods of time. Questions arise about the viability of production techniques using 3D printing for final products.

• Material limitations – A plastic replica will vary in strength based on the type of plastic material, which requires high temperatures for proper adhesion between the layers. Part strength cannot be measured when 3D printing is used for production. Metals are printed in layers that prove to have minute gaps, which affect the part's strength and performance. Specialized uses of glass and gold have been devised in companies with such needs, but these materials have not been commercialized for broad use.

• Accuracy questioned – 3D printing in the creation of a test part is considered acceptable in most fields. Final products that would be sold to consumers must follow exact specifications that can be duplicated thousands of times. 3D printers do not offer perfection when different materials are used to print the same part.

• Manufacturing feasibility – Prototype parts that are unique can be designed and printed in a matter of hours. Mass production of products through stamping and thermoforming requires less than one minute. 3D printing on a massive scale does not seem feasible in most manufacturing situations.

• Size limits – Small parts and objects can be printed in a matter of hours on a small 3D printer. Commercial 3D printers are expensive and require more space and raw material. Size limitations are presented since the build chamber is limited and the materials must have the strength to support the weight of the object as it is created. Large parts continue to present challenges for 3D printing.

14. Remarkable uses fo 3D printing

Innovative uses for 3D printing are surfacing when unique problems arise. Broad use of 3D printing will spread as more people realize that additive methods are within reach of individuals and companies. Creativity is limitless when a need is unique enough to require a new approach.

• Prosthetics for animals – Medicine applications for 3D printing have expanded to help animals with deformities. Certain situations were impossible to resolve in the past because of the massive design requirements for a prosthetic. The animal would die before the traditional design steps were completed.

•A bald eagle was shot in the beak by a poacher. The damage prevented the bird from eating, drinking and preening. A raptor expert was consulted to determine if a solution could be found. Scientists, engineers and a dentist rallied together to design a 3D beak, which saved the bird's life.

• A duckling hatched with his left foot backward. At the Feathered Angels Waterfowl Sanctuary, his foot was amputated and a 3D prosthesis was used to create a mold. A silicone duck foot was created to be soft enough for the duck to walk naturally. Instead of dragging himself around on his side and cutting his body, he will walk normally for the rest of his life.

• Art sculptures – For decades, artists have worked within constraints of materials and processes. 3D printing techniques have opened new doors to create intricate objects that were not possible up to now. Images on a computer screen can be changed to reflect the design the artist can visualize. 3D technology allows the CAD file to be converted into a cross section of slices that will be printed in attractive material. Post processing allows the artist to paint or resurface the printed object.

• Action figures – Polymers and plastics are two of the most common 3D printing materials that are readily available to consumers. Websites are acquiring designs that can be downloaded and printed on a 3D printer. Scanning an existing action figure presents special challenges because of concerns over copyright infringement. New characters can be created on sites like FigurePrints.

• Jewelry – Unique jewelry designs can be created in the CAD software and printed in wax. Plaster is poured on each side of the wax sculpture and allowed to dry to form a mold. Molten metal is poured into the mold opening in order to melt the wax and create the metal version of the jewelry piece. After solidifying and cooling, a jeweler will finish and polish the piece for sale to a customer. An infinite jewelry inventory is available to jewelers everywhere through this technique.

• Hearing aids – A 3D scanning wand is used to capture the dimensions of the patient's ear canal in a digital image. The hearing aid form is constructed to fit perfectly, which improves comfort and performance. Sound quality increases since the hearing device stays in place.

• Prototypes – Rapid improvements in each version of a product are possible because of the ease with which new prototypes can be created through 3D printing. Design characteristics can be changed on the computer and tested in a matter of hours, instead of weeks.

• Home décor – Objects that add interest and beauty to a tabletop, wall or shelf can be designed and printed with ease. Unique objects will traverse the path from concept through design and printing in a few hours. Various materials are available to offer texture and color combinations that complement existing décor.

• Models – Scale models of buildings, engines and other large objects can be created with the use of CAD software and a 3D printer. Anyone with clients who must see the object to be interested would benefit from a smaller version. Architects, real estate agents and automobile enthusiasts use 3D printing technology for many reasons.

• Component replacement – Broken parts can be replicated using a 3D scanner to create the CAD file. Appropriate materials are used in the 3D printer to produce the replacement. In some instances, a "part" is a knee replacement implant that is designed and printed specifically for the patient.

• Surgery preparation – An exact duplicate of a patient's scull can be scanned in 3D and printed to allow a surgeon to study a surgical procedure before performing it on the patient. This application is essential for surgeons who have to perform a complicated surgery for the first time. Printing bone grafts has become an important use of 3D printing technology following traumatic injuries.

• Reconstruction of a crime scene – Two-dimensional pictures allow the investigators to overlook important positional details that could might solve a crime. Specific details can be recreated through 3D printing to reveal crime solutions that were once considered hidden.